GW00993494

THE LITTLE BOOK OF WALES
LLYFR BACH CYMRU

Roger Thomas

First published in 2001
by Jarrold Publishing, Whitefriars,
Norwich NR3 1JR
Text © Roger Thomas
ISBN 0-7117-1612-9

This edition © Jarrold Publishing 2001, latest reprint 2004

Printed in China 3/04

Introduction

Wales is a small country full of surprises. And this is a small book full of fascinating facts which prove, once and for all, that Wales isn't a nation of coal mines and male voice choirs. The Welsh countryside changes with every mile. Deep valleys lead to long beaches, green hills rise into rocky mountains. This diversity also defines the personality of the country, as you'll discover from this book. Around 100 facts – some humorous and light-hearted, others thought-provoking and downright unbelievable – reveal the *real* Wales.

Radio waves

The world's first message transmitted by radio – 'Are you ready?' – was sent on 11 May 1897 by Guglielmo Marconi from Lavernock Point on the Glamorgan coast to Flat Holm island in the Bristol Channel, 3 miles (5 km) away.

TAKE A DEEP BREATH

The world's longest place name is to be found on the Isle of Anglesey.
The 58-letter ...
Llanfairpwllgwyngyllgogerychwyrn-drobwllllantysiliogogogoch means
'St Mary's (Church) by the white aspen over the whirlpool, and St Tysilio's (Church) by the red cave'.
So now you know!

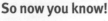

From small beginnings …

The National Trust was born in
Wales. In 1895 it was given its first
piece of land, the 4½-acre (1.8 ha)
Dinas Oleu headland ('The Fortress
of Light') overlooking Barmouth on
Cardigan Bay.

The mystery of the stones

No one has yet worked out how the 'bluestones' from the Preseli Hills in north Pembrokeshire were transported almost 200 miles (320 km) to Stonehenge on Salisbury Plain to be used in the construction of Britain's most famous prehistoric monument.

WALES/CYMRU

Wales derives from the Anglo-Saxon term *waleas*, meaning 'foreigner'. The country's Welsh name, *Cymru*, derives from the Celtic word *Cymry*, meaning 'fellow-countrymen'.

A cornucopia of castles

There are hundreds of castles in Wales – no one has managed to count them all – representing one of the highest concentrations of medieval fortifications in Europe.

Mountain high

The world's highest mountain is, in English, named after Sir George Everest (1790–1866), Surveyor-General of India. He lived at Gwernvale, a handsome house – now a hotel – on the edge of Crickhowell in the Brecon Beacons.

LITTLE ITALY

The Welsh have been enjoying authentic cappuccino and ice cream far longer than most other parts of Britain. Italian emigrants flocked to the industrial valleys of south Wales in the boom years of the 19th century, sensibly preferring to run cafés rather than work in the coal mines.

Shopping by catalogue – at the right Pryce!

It all began at Newtown in central Wales in 1859, when Sir Pryce Pryce-Jones started the world's first mail-order business.

The Welsh kilt

Yes, it does exist! Wales has its own national tartan, St David's, named after its patron saint. The pattern, the result of several years' research, can be seen on the Welsh kilt.

A BREEDING-GROUND FOR ACTORS

There must be something in the air around Port Talbot. The home town of Sir Anthony Hopkins is only a few miles from the village in which that other great Welsh actor, Richard Burton, was born. Also close by is Neath, where 1940s Hollywood heart-throb and Oscar-winner Ray Milland was born.

In search of the Holy Grail

For many years, the cup used by Christ in the Last Supper was said to have been kept at Nanteos, a Georgian mansion – now a hotel – near Aberystwyth. It was reputedly brought to Nanteos by the monks of nearby Strata Florida Abbey.

THE FIRST BOOK

Tales passed by word of mouth in the Wales of the Dark Ages were written down in medieval times. The collection of stories is known as the *Mabinogion*. The earliest surviving manuscripts, from the 14th century, are in the National Library of Wales at Aberystwyth.

Mining disaster

The worst mining disaster in Wales took place at the Universal Colliery, Senghenydd, in 1913, when 439 men and boys were killed.

THE LAST MINE

In the heyday of coal mining there were hundreds of pits in industrial south Wales employing thousands of people. Now, only one working mine remains – Tower colliery, near Hirwaun, run as a co-operative by the miners themselves.

THE PAST REMEMBERED

The small south Wales town of Blaenavon has become a member of an exclusive club, one of only 25 Unesco World Heritage Sites in Britain. It joins Hadrian's Wall, Stonehenge and Canterbury Cathedral on the strength of its outstanding industrial heritage – its old ironworks and coal mine are open to visitors.

Highest waterfall

Wales's (and England's) highest waterfall is the 240-foot (73 m) Pistyll Rhaeadr near Llanrhaeadr ym Mochnant.

The village of the future

The Centre for Alternative Technology near Machynlleth is almost self-sufficient. It's the ultimate 'green' village, relying on aerogenerators, waterwheels, solar panels and other ingenious energy-saving devices.

THE 'SANDS OF SPEED'

Pendine's vast beach, stretching for 6 miles (9.7 km), was used for land speed record attempts in the 1920s. Sir Malcolm Campbell became the world's fastest man on four wheels when he drove *Blue Bird* here at over 170 mph (274 kph).

WALKING HAND-IN-HAND

A favourite walk for romantic couples on the Isle of Anglesey takes them along the beach to the rocky promontory of Llanddwyn Island and the ruins of a church dedicated to St Dwynwen, patron saint of lovers.

Symbol of love

Forget engagement rings. The traditional symbol of betrothal in Wales is the lovespoon, intricately carved from a single piece of wood.

The last native leader

Owain Glyndŵr is generally
recognised as Wales's last native
leader. He led an uprising against
England in the early 15th century and
established Welsh parliaments at
Machynlleth, Harlech and Dolgellau.
A mercurial figure, he disappeared in
around 1412 never to be seen again.

Fan club

One of Dylan Thomas's biggest fans is ex-US President Jimmy Carter. He opened the Dylan Thomas Centre at the poet's home town of Swansea.

TIME WARP

The inhabitants of Pembrokeshire's Gwaun valley are literally living in the past. They still celebrate New Year on 13 January, adhering to the old pre-1752 calendar.

Coastal splendour

Pembrokeshire is home to Britain's only coastal-based National Park. Its symbol, the razorbill, reflects Pembrokeshire's teeming populations of seabirds.

A medieval bottleneck

Monmouth has the only bridge in Britain fortified with a gatehouse. The 13th-century Monnow Bridge is still fulfilling its original purpose of impeding entry into the town – nowadays it's a notorious bottleneck for cars and trucks.

Monmouth's famous sons

Charles Stewart Rolls, co-founder of Rolls-Royce, was the first Briton to be killed in a flying accident. This pioneer aviator, driver and balloonist, who died in 1910, came from Monmouth. His statue stands in Agincourt Square, close to that of another famous son, Henry V, victor at the Battle of Agincourt of 1415.

SEAWEED FOR BREAKFAST!

The traditional Welsh delicacy known as laver bread is tastier than it looks. Black and gooey, this puréed form of seaweed is usually eaten with bacon and eggs.

Largest Lake

Four-mile-long (6.4 km) Bala Lake, or Llyn Tegid, is the largest natural lake in Wales. It is home to the elusive gwyniad, a species of fish reputedly unique to the lake.

Almost a quarter ...

Between them, Wales's three National Parks and five 'Areas of Outstanding Natural Beauty' cover 23% of the country.

A LIVING LANGUAGE

Around 18% of Wales's population of 2.8 million can speak Welsh.

FLYING THE FLAG

No one really knows how the red
dragon came to be the emblem for the
Welsh flag. It may have been the battle
standard of the early Britons after the
Roman occupation. An 8th-century
legend tells of a fight between a red
dragon (Wales) and white dragon
(England) in which the former
triumphed.

THE LEEK

Wales's national emblem is the leek. It was reputedly adopted after a battle in which Welsh forces wore leeks in their hats to distinguish themselves from the English enemy. This tradition, of course, has absolutely nothing to do with the wearing of leeks during Wales–England rugby internationals!

Leek versus daffodil

Wales has another national emblem – the daffodil. This may be because the Welsh word for leek – *cenhinen* – is almost the same as daffodil (*cenhinen pedr*). St David's Day, 1 March, is celebrated by wearing the leek or daffodil.

Highest rainfall

The summit of Snowdon has the highest rainfall in Wales, with an average of 180 inches (4,570 mm) a year.

THE NATIONAL SPORT

Wales's obsession with a certain team game involving red jerseys and a strangely shaped ball can be traced back to the Castle Hotel, Neath, which was the venue for the inaugural meeting of the Welsh Rugby Union in 1881. The first game was played in 1850, at St David's College, Lampeter.

SQUEAKING SANDS

The 'Whistling Sands' at Porth Oer on the Llŷn peninsula really do squeak underfoot, a noise caused by the grains rubbing together under compression.

Deepest

Britain's deepest cave, descending 1,010 feet (308 m), is Ogof Fynnon Ddu near Abercraf in the upper Tawe valley. It goes on for 28 miles (45 km), making it the second-longest cave in Britain.

Sunniest – and windiest!

The exposed Dale peninsula in south-west Pembrokeshire is the sunniest place in Wales, with an annual average of over 1,800 hours. It's also the windiest, with speeds of over 100 mph (160 kph) having been recorded.

FULL STEAM AHEAD

Contrary to popular belief, George Stephenson's *Rocket* wasn't the world's first steam train. Invented by Richard Trevithick, the first ran 10 miles (16 km) from Merthyr Tydfil to Abercynon in 1804, beating the *Rocket* by over twenty years.

THE SMALLEST TRAIN

Wales is famous for its steam-powered 'little railways'. The smallest is the Fairbourne and Barmouth Steam Railway, which runs on the narrowest of narrow gauges – a tiny 12¼ inches (31.11 cm) – for 2 miles (3.2 km) from Fairbourne to the mouth of the Mawddach estuary.

Lawrence of Wales

T.E. Lawrence, better known as Lawrence of Arabia, was born in Tremadog, north Wales, in 1888.

HIGHEST AND WETTEST

The wettest place in Wales also happens to be the highest mountain in Britain south of the Scottish Highlands. Snowdon stands at 3,560 feet (1,085 m), one of fifteen peaks in Wales over 3,000 feet (914 m).

The ugliest house in Wales?

Surely not. The Ugly House, an old cottage outside Betws-y-Coed built of misshapen, massive boulders, is positively picturesque in comparison to the architectural monstrosities of the 20th century.

THE SMALLEST HOUSE

This toytown dwelling, just 9 feet
(2.7 m) high by 6 feet (1.8 m) wide,
stands on the quay at Conwy.
Unbelievably, Britain's smallest
house was once home to a fisherman
6 feet 3 inches (1.9 m) tall!

The first castle?

Experts believe that Britain's first stone castle was built at Chepstow. Begun just one year after the Norman Conquest of 1066, it marks a major transition in castle design – the end of the rough-and-ready strongholds made from earth and timber, and the beginning of powerful, stone-built fortresses.

THE 'SLEEPING GIANT'

Britain's second-largest castle is located in Caerphilly, near Cardiff. This 'undiscovered' masterpiece of military architecture covers 30 acres (12ha), only slightly smaller than Dover Castle's 34 acres (14ha).

A GOOD READ

At the last count, there were over thirty bookshops in Hay-on-Wye, making this small border town the 'second-hand book capital of the world'.

Heavy burial

The massive 40-ton capstone crowning the Tinkinswood Burial Chamber in the Vale of Glamorgan is the largest in Britain. How did our prehistoric ancestors ever manage to shift it?

All things being equal =

The equal sign in mathematics was invented by Robert Recorde of Tenby, a brilliant 16th-century academic.

HAPPY CAMPERS

Camping holidays were invented in Wales in 1802 when Thomas de Quincey toured the country, staying in a tent.

Making an impression

It's a little-known fact that the National Museum and Gallery in Cardiff has the best collection of Impressionist and Post-Impressionist art outside France. Monet, Cézanne, Van Gogh and Renoir are amongst the artists represented.

The world's first hippy?

Dr William Price (1800–93) was a man born before his time. This charismatic character, who wore a fox fur on his head, was an advocate of vegetarianism, nudism and free love. He was pro-environment and anti-smoking, and was instrumental in making cremation legal in Britain.

GHOST VILLAGE REBORN

When quarrying ceased, the remote village of Nant Gwytheyrn on the Llŷn peninsula, accessible only by a steep track through the cliffs, was abandoned. Nowadays it has a new lease of life as a centre for Welsh-language studies.

The first eisteddfod

Wales's first eisteddfod (cultural folk gathering) took place at Cardigan Castle in 1176. The first 'modern' eisteddfod was held at Corwen in 1789.

YALE'S RESTING-PLACE

The benefactor Elihu Yale (1648–1721), who helped found the great American university that bears his name, is buried at Wrexham's Church of St Giles. A long epitaph on his tomb begins: 'Born in America, in Europe Bred'.

O LITTLE TOWN
OF BETHLEHEM

The hamlet of Bethlehem near Llandeilo has a busy little post office – especially during the franking of Christmas mail and first-day covers.

Highest road

The highest mountain road in Wales is Bwlch y Groes ('The Pass of the Cross'), rising to 1,790 feet (545 m) between Dinas Mawddwy and Bala Lake.

Roman Gold rush

Pumsaint, deep in the hills between Llandovery and Lampeter, is the only spot in Britain where we know, for certain, that the Romans mined for gold. Evidence of the sophisticated methods they used can still be seen.

WELSH GOLD RUSH

In the 19th century the staid country town of Dolgellau turned into a Klondike when prospectors arrived in search of Welsh gold. It's still there – one family recently paid for their holiday by panning for gold in the River Mawddach.

Hot house

The new National Botanic Garden of Wales in the Vale of Tywi, near Carmarthen, has the world's largest single-span glasshouse, 312 feet (95 m) long by 180 feet (55 m) wide, glazed with over 48,000 square feet (4,500 sq m) of glass.

Working class

Wales was the first nation in the world to employ more people in industry than agriculture.

A FOOT IN THE DOOR …

In 1900, Scotsman Keir Hardie became Britain's first Labour MP when he was elected to represent Merthyr Tydfil.

FACT OR FICTION?

When St David, Wales's patron saint, addressed a religious gathering in Llanddewi Brefi, near Tregaron, in AD 519, the ground is said to have risen beneath his feet so that he could be better seen and heard. This legend may have something to do with the fact that the village's Church of St David stands on a prominent mound above the streets!

High and dry

Centuries ago, the outcrop of Craig-yr-Aderyn, near Tywyn, was lapped by the waves of Cardigan Bay. As the waters receded, this former sea-cliff was left landlocked, 4 miles (6.4 km) from the coast. No one told the seabirds – they still happily nest there, giving Craig-yr-Aderyn its name, which means 'Bird Rock'.

Space to breathe

Just 5% of the British population lives in Wales, while London accounts for around 12%!

GONE FISHING

The coracle, a tiny one-man fishing-boat that looks like an upturned umbrella and has been in use in Wales for over 2,000 years, can still be seen on the waters of the River Teifi.

Counting sheep

Sheep outnumber people in Wales by four to one – which means that there are over 10 million sheep in Wales! Welshpool's Monday sheep market is said to be the largest in Europe.

Ghostly border

The 'little England beyond Wales' of
south Pembrokeshire and the more
traditionally Welsh north are divided
by the mysterious Landsker line.
Although it doesn't appear on any
map, the locals know precisely where
it is.

THE LAST INVASION OF BRITAIN

This farcical affair took place in February 1797 when an ill-prepared force of French troops, led by an American general, landed near Fishguard. They were seen off by the locals. One lady, the formidable Jemima Nicholas, armed with only a pitchfork, captured twelve Frenchmen! The event is recorded on a tapestry in the town.

LONGEST FOOTPATH

Wales's longest continuous footpath is the 186-mile (299 km) Pembrokeshire Coast Path, which runs from Amroth in the south to the mouth of the River Teifi on Cardigan Bay.

Longest aqueduct

The 1,006-foot (307 m) Pontcysyllte
Aqueduct, which carries the
Llangollen Canal across the Vale of
Dee, is the longest in Britain.

IN SEARCH OF CAMELOT

One of the sites which claims to be the setting of King Arthur's fabled round table is the Roman amphitheatre at Caerleon. At least it's the right shape!

Merlin's Oak

They're living dangerously in Carmarthen. The town, reputedly the birthplace of Merlin the Magician, has removed the wizened tree known as Merlin's Oak despite the prophecy:

*When Merlin's Oak shall
 tumble down,
Then shall fall Carmarthen town.*

Water, water everywhere

Although less than 150 miles (240 km) from north to south, there are over 15,000 miles (24,140 km) of rivers and around 500 lakes in Wales.

THE GREAT WELSH DESERT

The dune system at Merthyr Mawr on the Glamorgan coast is the largest in Europe. The dunes themselves rise to over 200 feet (61 m).

Longest beach

The 7-mile (11.3 km) beach at Cefn Sidan on Carmarthen Bay is the longest in Wales.

SHE'S NO LADY

The 'Red Lady of Paviland' is a man. The bones of the 'Lady', dating back some 23,000 years, are some of the oldest remains of *Homo sapiens* found in Britain. On closer inspection, the remains, unearthed in a cave on the Gower peninsula in 1823, were discovered to be those of a man.

Bird-life

Britain's first bird observatory was established on Skokholm island off the Pembrokeshire coast in 1933.

BLACK GOLD

In 1913, Cardiff became the world's busiest coal-exporting port, despatching over 10 million tons of 'black gold'.

The Norwegian connection

Roald Dahl, the writer of spooky children's stories, was born in Cardiff. His father, a wealthy Norwegian merchant, had his son baptised in Cardiff Bay's Norwegian Church, which is now an arts centre and café.

The Atlantic by air

The first non-stop flight across the Atlantic from Britain to the USA was made by Amy Johnson and Jim Mollison in July 1933. They took off from Pendine on Carmarthen Bay and landed 34 hours later.

OUT OF AFRICA

The Zulu Room in the South Wales Borderers' Museum, Brecon, is packed full of memorabilia from the regiment's defence of Rorke's Drift in 1879, when it held out against 4,000 warriors. The battle became the subject of *Zulu*, an early Michael Caine film.

It's beautiful – and that's official!

In 1956, the Gower peninsula in south Wales was the first part of Britain to be declared an official 'Area of Outstanding Natural Beauty'.

THE WELSH ROBIN HOOD

In the 16th century the outlaw Twm Siôn Cati hid from the Sheriff of Carmarthen in a cave deep in the hills north of Llandovery. It's still there – see if you can find it on Dinas Hill above the tumbling River Tywi.

Boiling point

According to legend, in the 18th century, runner Guto Nyth Bran ran across the mountain from Llanwonno above Pontypridd in the time it took to boil a kettle of water.

Rare plant

The limestone outcrops north of Merthyr Tydfil are the only place in the world where you'll see the plant known as Ley's whitebeam.

Medieval prescription 1

'If thou desirest to die, eat cabbage in August.'

The Physicians of Myddfai

MEDIEVAL PRESCRIPTION 2

'Suppers kill more than the Physicians of Myddfai can cure.'

The first Tudor king

The mighty Tudor dynasty of English monarchs sprung from Welsh roots. Welshman Harri Tudur became Henry VII, first of the Tudors, when he won a famous victory over Richard III at the Battle of Bosworth in 1485.

Hot spot

The highest temperature ever recorded in Wales was 35.2° C (95.4° F) at Hawarden Bridge on 2 August 1990.

LET THE TRAIN TAKE THE STRAIN

Mountaineering is made easy on the rack-and-pinion Snowdon Mountain Railway, Britain's loftiest train ride, which takes you to the highest summit in England and Wales.

AN EVENTFUL PLACE

Llanwrtyd Wells claims to be the smallest town in Britain. It's very good at self-promotion – its unusual programme of annual events includes a 'Man versus Horse' marathon and International Bog-Snorkelling in a local peat bog!

An overcrowded island

The tiny island of Grassholm off the
Pembrokeshire coast is home to
around 30,000 pairs of gannets, the
fourth-largest population of such
birds in the world.

Sea view

William Randolph Hearst, the American newspaper tycoon who built the fabulous San Simeon Castle on the Californian coast, must have liked sea views. In the 1930s he also restored St Donat's Castle on the Glamorgan Heritage Coast.

COMEBACK

The red kite, once almost extinct in Britain, has made a comeback in the remote Welsh hills. The Cambrian Mountains are now home to over 200 breeding pairs of this rare bird of prey.

BIG BOG

Cors Caron, or Tregaron Bog, is the largest in Wales. It's also an important National Nature Reserve with a flourishing wildlife, and a good place to spot the rare red kite.

Beware of Blackadder!

Watch your step when exploring Tregaron Bog. It's the British black adder's only habitat.

TRAINING GROUND

Sir Edmund Hillary and his team used the rocky slopes of Snowdonia as a training ground prior to the first successful assault on Mount Everest in 1953. Memorabilia from the team can be seen at the Pen-y-Gwryd Inn, a famous climbing hostelry at the foot of Snowdon.